50 Premium Ramen Noodle Dishes

By: Kelly Johnson

Table of Contents

- Tonkotsu Black Garlic Ramen
- Miso Butter Corn Ramen
- Spicy Tan Tan Ramen
- Shoyu Truffle Ramen
- Tsukemen Dipping Ramen
- Vegan Mushroom Umami Ramen
- Chicken Paitan Ramen
- Spicy Kimchi Pork Ramen
- Lobster Miso Ramen
- Wagyu Beef Ramen
- Duck Confit Ramen
- Shrimp Tempura Ramen
- Curry Coconut Ramen
- Cold Sesame Ramen
- Yuzu Shio Ramen
- Spicy Seafood Ramen
- Chashu Pork Belly Ramen

- Green Tea Matcha Ramen
- Black Sesame Chicken Ramen
- Clam and Kombu Ramen
- Roasted Garlic Miso Ramen
- Crispy Tofu Szechuan Ramen
- Uni Cream Ramen
- Teriyaki Chicken Ramen
- Thai Tom Yum Ramen
- BBQ Short Rib Ramen
- Sweet Chili Tofu Ramen
- Bacon and Egg Breakfast Ramen
- Spicy Gochujang Ramen
- Smoked Salmon Cream Ramen
- Honey Soy Glazed Ramen
- Wild Mushroom Truffle Ramen
- Braised Oxtail Ramen
- Lemongrass Chicken Ramen
- Sesame Chili Oil Ramen
- Soft Shell Crab Ramen

- Roasted Duck Miso Ramen
- Bulgogi Beef Ramen
- Charred Corn & Bacon Ramen
- Ginger Scallion Ramen
- Sake-Steamed Clam Ramen
- Kimchi Cheese Ramen
- Tempura Vegetable Ramen
- Oyster Cream Ramen
- Roasted Tomato Basil Ramen
- Maple Miso Glazed Ramen
- Chili Lime Chicken Ramen
- Garlic Butter Shrimp Ramen
- Tofu & Avocado Ramen
- Spicy Black Bean Ramen

Tonkotsu Black Garlic Ramen

Broth:

- 2 lbs pork bones (neck and femur)
- 1 onion (halved)
- 1 head garlic (halved)
- 2-inch ginger (sliced)
- 1 leek (cut into chunks)
- 10 cups water
- Simmer for 12+ hours, skimming impurities.

Black Garlic Oil:

- 1/2 cup neutral oil
- 6 cloves black garlic
- 2 cloves regular garlic
- Blend garlic, heat gently in oil until fragrant. Strain.

Toppings:

- Chashu pork
- Soft-boiled eggs
- Green onions
- Bamboo shoots

- Nori

Assembly:

1. Cook ramen noodles.

2. Add broth to bowl, drizzle black garlic oil.

3. Top with noodles, pork, egg, and garnishes.

Miso Butter Corn Ramen

Broth:

- 4 cups chicken stock
- 2 tbsp white miso paste
- 1 tbsp red miso paste
- 1 tbsp soy sauce
- 1 tsp sesame oil
- 1 clove garlic (minced)
- 1 tsp grated ginger
- Simmer for 15 min.

Toppings:

- 1 tbsp butter (per bowl)
- Sweet corn
- Green onions
- Bean sprouts
- Soft-boiled egg
- Toasted sesame seeds

Assembly:

1. Cook ramen noodles.

2. Add butter and ladle broth over.

3. Top with corn, sprouts, egg, and green onions.

Spicy Tan Tan Ramen

Broth:

- 3 cups chicken broth
- 1 cup soy milk
- 2 tbsp tahini
- 1 tbsp doubanjiang (fermented bean paste)
- 1 tbsp chili oil
- 1 clove garlic (minced)
- 1 tsp grated ginger

Toppings:

- Spicy ground pork (sautéed with soy sauce, sake, and sugar)
- Bok choy
- Green onions
- Soft-boiled egg
- Chili oil drizzle

Assembly:

1. Blend broth ingredients until smooth, heat gently.
2. Cook ramen noodles.
3. Pour broth, top with pork, bok choy, egg, and chili oil.

Shoyu Truffle Ramen

Broth:

- 4 cups chicken broth
- 2 cups dashi
- 3 tbsp soy sauce
- 1 tbsp mirin
- 1 tsp sugar

Truffle Essence:

- 1/2 tsp truffle oil per bowl (add just before serving)

Toppings:

- Sliced chicken breast or chashu
- Soft-boiled egg
- Green onions
- Menma (bamboo shoots)
- Nori

Assembly:

1. Heat broth.
2. Cook ramen noodles.
3. Pour broth, drizzle truffle oil, add toppings.

Tsukemen Dipping Ramen

Broth (Dipping Sauce):

- 2 cups dashi
- 1/2 cup soy sauce
- 1/4 cup mirin
- 1 tbsp rice vinegar
- 1 tsp sugar
- Bonito flakes
- Simmer and strain.

Toppings:

- Chashu pork slices
- Nori
- Soft-boiled egg
- Green onions
- Lime wedge

Assembly:

1. Cook and chill thick ramen noodles.
2. Serve dipping broth hot or warm in a separate bowl.
3. Dip noodles, enjoy with toppings.

Vegan Mushroom Umami Ramen

Broth:

- 6 cups water
- 1 sheet kombu
- 1/2 cup dried shiitake mushrooms
- 1 tbsp white miso
- 1 tbsp soy sauce
- 1 tsp sesame oil
- Simmer 30 min, strain kombu.

Toppings:

- Grilled king oyster mushrooms
- Corn
- Bok choy
- Green onions
- Tofu
- Chili oil (optional)

Assembly:

1. Cook ramen noodles.
2. Add broth to bowl, top with veggies and tofu.

Chicken Paitan Ramen

Broth:

- 2 lbs chicken wings and carcasses
- 1 onion
- 2-inch ginger
- Water to cover
- Simmer 6–8 hours until cloudy.

Tare (Seasoning Sauce):

- 2 tbsp soy sauce
- 1 tbsp mirin
- 1/2 tsp salt

Toppings:

- Poached chicken breast
- Green onions
- Soft-boiled egg
- Corn
- Nori

Assembly:

1. Mix tare into broth.

2. Cook ramen noodles.

3. Assemble with chicken, egg, and garnishes.

Spicy Kimchi Pork Ramen

Broth:

- 4 cups pork or chicken broth
- 1 cup kimchi (chopped)
- 1 tbsp gochujang (Korean chili paste)
- 1 tbsp soy sauce
- 1 tsp sesame oil
- Garlic & ginger (minced)

Toppings:

- Sautéed ground pork
- Extra kimchi
- Green onions
- Soft-boiled egg
- Bean sprouts

Assembly:

1. Cook ramen noodles.
2. Simmer broth with kimchi and gochujang.
3. Pour broth, top with pork, sprouts, and egg.

Lobster Miso Ramen

Broth:

- Lobster shells from 1–2 lobsters
- 1 tbsp white miso paste
- 4 cups seafood or chicken stock
- 1-inch ginger, sliced
- 1 clove garlic, crushed
- 1 tbsp sake
- Simmer shells in stock 1 hour, strain, whisk in miso.

Toppings:

- Lobster meat (poached or sautéed in butter)
- Soft-boiled egg
- Sweet corn
- Green onions
- Nori

Assembly:

1. Cook ramen noodles.
2. Pour broth, top with lobster, corn, egg, and garnishes.

Wagyu Beef Ramen

Broth:

- 4 cups beef broth
- 2 cups dashi
- 1 tbsp soy sauce
- 1 tsp mirin
- 1 garlic clove, smashed

Toppings:

- Thinly sliced Wagyu (lightly torched or seared)
- Soft-boiled egg
- Green onions
- Enoki mushrooms
- Truffle oil (optional)

Assembly:

1. Cook ramen noodles.
2. Pour broth into bowl.
3. Lay beef slices on top, add other garnishes.

Duck Confit Ramen

Broth:

- 4 cups duck or chicken broth
- 1 tbsp soy sauce
- 1 tbsp hoisin sauce
- 1 tsp sesame oil
- 1-inch ginger, sliced

Toppings:

- Shredded duck confit
- Baby spinach
- Soft-boiled egg
- Pickled shiitake mushrooms
- Green onions

Assembly:

1. Heat and season broth.
2. Cook noodles, add to bowl.
3. Top with duck and garnishes.

Shrimp Tempura Ramen

Broth:

- 4 cups dashi or seafood broth
- 1 tbsp soy sauce
- 1 tsp mirin
- 1 tsp grated ginger

Toppings:

- Shrimp tempura (crispy)
- Green onions
- Soft-boiled egg
- Shredded nori
- Daikon oroshi (optional)

Assembly:

1. Cook noodles and place in bowl.
2. Add hot broth.
3. Top with crispy shrimp and other ingredients right before serving.

Curry Coconut Ramen

Broth:

- 1 tbsp red curry paste
- 1 cup coconut milk
- 3 cups chicken or veggie broth
- 1 tsp fish sauce
- 1 tsp brown sugar
- Lime juice to finish

Toppings:

- Grilled chicken or tofu
- Bean sprouts
- Cilantro
- Lime wedge
- Soft-boiled egg

Assembly:

1. Sauté curry paste, add broth and coconut milk, simmer.
2. Cook ramen noodles.
3. Combine in bowl, add toppings.

Cold Sesame Ramen (Hiyashi Chuka Style)

Sauce:

- 2 tbsp tahini
- 1 tbsp soy sauce
- 1 tsp rice vinegar
- 1 tsp sesame oil
- 1/2 tsp sugar
- Water to thin

Toppings:

- Cucumber (julienned)
- Carrot (julienned)
- Tomato slices
- Boiled egg halves
- Cold shredded chicken or tofu
- Sesame seeds

Assembly:

1. Cook ramen noodles, rinse in cold water.
2. Mix with sauce, top with veggies and protein.

Yuzu Shio Ramen

Broth:

- 4 cups chicken broth
- 1 cup dashi
- 1 tbsp yuzu juice
- 1 tsp salt
- 1/2 tsp soy sauce (optional)
- Yuzu zest (pinch)

Toppings:

- Sliced chicken breast
- Green onions
- Nori
- Bamboo shoots
- Soft-boiled egg

Assembly:

1. Heat broth gently.
2. Cook noodles, add to bowl.
3. Add chicken and garnishes, finish with yuzu juice and zest.

Spicy Seafood Ramen

Broth:

- 4 cups seafood broth
- 1 tbsp gochujang (Korean chili paste)
- 1 tsp soy sauce
- 1 tsp fish sauce
- Garlic and ginger (minced)
- Chili oil to taste

Toppings:

- Shrimp, squid, mussels
- Bok choy
- Soft-boiled egg
- Scallions
- Nori

Assembly:

1. Sauté seafood briefly, set aside.
2. Simmer broth with seasonings.
3. Cook noodles, add broth, top with seafood and veggies.

Chashu Pork Belly Ramen

Broth:

- 6 cups pork or chicken stock
- 2 tbsp soy sauce
- 1 tbsp mirin
- 1 tsp sake
- 1 clove garlic (smashed)
- 1-inch ginger (sliced)
- Simmer for 1 hour.

Chashu Pork Belly:

- Roll pork belly and tie.
- Braise in soy sauce, sake, mirin, sugar, and ginger for 2 hours.
- Slice thinly.

Toppings:

- Soft-boiled egg
- Bamboo shoots
- Green onions
- Nori
- Chashu slices

Assembly:

1. Cook ramen noodles.
2. Add broth, top with pork, egg, and garnishes.

Green Tea Matcha Ramen

Broth:

- 4 cups light vegetable or chicken broth
- 1 tsp matcha powder (sifted)
- 1 tbsp white miso
- Whisk until smooth, heat gently.

Toppings:

- Steamed spinach
- Soft-boiled egg
- Tofu or chicken
- Sesame seeds
- Green onions

Assembly:

1. Cook matcha soba or ramen noodles (or add a pinch of matcha to boiling water).
2. Combine with broth, top with greens and protein.

Black Sesame Chicken Ramen

Broth:

- 4 cups chicken broth
- 2 tbsp black sesame paste
- 1 tbsp soy sauce
- 1 clove garlic (minced)
- Blend and simmer.

Toppings:

- Grilled or seared chicken thigh
- Soft-boiled egg
- Spinach or bok choy
- Black sesame seeds
- Scallions

Assembly:

1. Cook ramen noodles.
2. Pour black sesame broth, top with chicken and garnishes.

Clam and Kombu Ramen

Broth:

- 2 cups kombu dashi
- 2 cups clam juice
- 1/2 cup sake
- 1 tbsp soy sauce
- 1 tsp mirin
- Simmer gently with clams until they open, remove clams.

Toppings:

- Steamed clams
- Green onions
- Wakame seaweed
- Nori
- Lime wedge

Assembly:

1. Cook ramen noodles.
2. Add broth, top with clams and garnishes.

Roasted Garlic Miso Ramen

Broth:

- 4 cups chicken broth
- 2 tbsp white miso
- 1 whole garlic bulb (roasted and mashed)
- 1 tsp soy sauce
- 1 tsp sesame oil
- Simmer all ingredients.

Toppings:

- Roasted garlic cloves
- Soft-boiled egg
- Corn
- Chashu or chicken
- Green onions

Assembly:

1. Cook ramen noodles.
2. Add to bowl with garlic-rich miso broth, top generously.

Crispy Tofu Szechuan Ramen

Broth:

- 4 cups vegetable broth
- 1 tbsp doubanjiang (spicy bean paste)
- 1 tsp soy sauce
- 1 tsp black vinegar
- 1 tsp Sichuan pepper oil
- Simmer with garlic and ginger.

Crispy Tofu:

- Cube firm tofu, coat lightly in cornstarch, and fry until golden.

Toppings:

- Baby bok choy
- Bean sprouts
- Green onions
- Chili crisp
- Crispy tofu cubes

Assembly:

1. Cook ramen noodles.
2. Pour spicy broth, add tofu and toppings.

Uni Cream Ramen

Broth:

- 1/2 cup heavy cream
- 1/4 cup seafood stock
- 2 tbsp uni (sea urchin roe)
- 1 tsp soy sauce
- Blend into a smooth emulsion, warm gently.

Toppings:

- Extra fresh uni
- Shiso leaf or nori
- Soft-boiled egg
- Salmon roe (optional)
- Scallions

Assembly:

1. Cook ramen noodles.
2. Pour uni cream over noodles, top delicately with uni and garnishes.

Teriyaki Chicken Ramen

Broth:

- 4 cups chicken broth
- 1 tbsp soy sauce
- 1 tsp mirin
- 1 tsp brown sugar
- Garlic and ginger (lightly sautéed)

Teriyaki Chicken:

- Grill chicken thigh and glaze with teriyaki sauce (soy, mirin, sugar, sake).

Toppings:

- Sliced teriyaki chicken
- Corn
- Green onions
- Soft-boiled egg
- Toasted sesame seeds

Assembly:

1. Cook ramen noodles.
2. Pour in broth, top with glazed chicken and garnishes.

Thai Tom Yum Ramen

Broth:

- 4 cups chicken or seafood broth
- 2 stalks lemongrass (smashed)
- 3 kaffir lime leaves
- 1-inch galangal (sliced)
- 2 tbsp Tom Yum paste
- 1 tbsp fish sauce
- 1 tsp sugar
- 1 tbsp lime juice
- Optional: 1–2 Thai chilies

Toppings:

- Shrimp or chicken
- Mushrooms (straw or shiitake)
- Cilantro
- Bean sprouts
- Lime wedge

Assembly:

1. Simmer broth with aromatics, strain, season with paste and lime.

2. Cook noodles, combine with broth, and top with seafood and garnishes.

BBQ Short Rib Ramen

Broth:

- 4 cups beef broth
- 1/2 cup dashi
- 1 tbsp soy sauce
- 1 tsp garlic
- 1 tbsp mirin

Short Ribs:

- Slow braise ribs in soy, mirin, garlic, brown sugar until tender.
- Grill or broil for caramelization.

Toppings:

- Sliced short rib
- Soft-boiled egg
- Green onions
- Pickled onions
- Nori

Assembly:

1. Cook ramen noodles.
2. Pour broth, top with ribs and garnishes.

Sweet Chili Tofu Ramen

Broth:

- 4 cups veggie broth
- 1 tbsp soy sauce
- 1 tsp rice vinegar
- 1 tsp chili garlic sauce
- 1 tsp sesame oil

Tofu:

- Pan-fry tofu cubes, glaze with sweet chili sauce.

Toppings:

- Tofu
- Carrot ribbons
- Cilantro
- Crushed peanuts
- Lime wedge

Assembly:

1. Cook ramen noodles.
2. Add sweet-savory broth, top with tofu and crunchy toppings.

Bacon and Egg Breakfast Ramen

Broth:

- 4 cups chicken broth
- 1 tbsp soy sauce
- 1 tsp maple syrup (optional)
- Dash of black pepper

Toppings:

- Crispy bacon strips
- Soft-boiled or poached egg
- Sautéed spinach
- Green onions
- Optional: hash brown bites or fried shallots

Assembly:

1. Cook ramen noodles.
2. Add broth, then layer on bacon and breakfast garnishes.

Spicy Gochujang Ramen

Broth:

- 4 cups chicken broth
- 1 tbsp gochujang
- 1 tsp soy sauce
- 1/2 tsp sesame oil
- 1 clove garlic (minced)
- 1/2 tsp sugar

Toppings:

- Sautéed ground pork or tofu
- Bok choy
- Green onions
- Soft-boiled egg
- Chili oil drizzle

Assembly:

1. Simmer broth until gochujang dissolves.
2. Cook ramen noodles and top with spicy elements.

Smoked Salmon Cream Ramen

Broth:

- 1/2 cup heavy cream
- 1/2 cup milk
- 2 cups light fish or chicken broth
- 1 tsp lemon juice
- Salt & white pepper to taste

Toppings:

- Smoked salmon slices
- Dill
- Capers (optional)
- Soft-boiled egg
- Microgreens

Assembly:

1. Warm broth until creamy.
2. Cook ramen noodles, top with salmon and garnish like a creamy lox bagel.

Honey Soy Glazed Ramen

Broth:

- 4 cups chicken broth
- 1 tbsp soy sauce
- 1 tsp rice vinegar
- 1 tsp sesame oil

Glaze:

- Mix 2 tbsp soy sauce, 1 tbsp honey, 1 tsp garlic, 1/2 tsp chili flakes.
- Glaze grilled chicken or tofu.

Toppings:

- Honey soy glazed protein
- Green onions
- Sesame seeds
- Soft-boiled egg
- Pickled radish

Assembly:

1. Cook ramen noodles.
2. Pour broth, top with glazed slices and fresh toppings.

Wild Mushroom Truffle Ramen

Broth:

- 4 cups mushroom or vegetable broth
- 1 tbsp soy sauce
- 1 tsp white miso
- 1 tsp truffle oil (add at the end)

Toppings:

- Sautéed wild mushrooms (shiitake, oyster, maitake)
- Soft-boiled egg
- Scallions
- Microgreens
- Parmesan (optional)

Assembly:

1. Cook noodles.
2. Add earthy broth and elegant toppings, drizzle with truffle oil.

Braised Oxtail Ramen

Broth:

- 4 oxtail pieces, seared
- 6 cups beef stock
- 1 onion, halved
- 1-inch ginger, sliced
- 1 clove garlic
- 1 tbsp soy sauce
- Simmer 3–4 hours, strain.

Toppings:

- Shredded braised oxtail
- Soft-boiled egg
- Pickled radish
- Scallions
- Nori

Assembly:

1. Cook ramen noodles.
2. Add rich broth, top with tender oxtail and garnishes.

Lemongrass Chicken Ramen

Broth:

- 4 cups chicken broth
- 2 lemongrass stalks (smashed)
- 1-inch ginger
- 1 clove garlic
- 1 tsp fish sauce
- 1 tsp lime juice
- Simmer and strain.

Toppings:

- Grilled lemongrass-marinated chicken
- Cilantro
- Bean sprouts
- Lime wedge
- Chili flakes

Assembly:

1. Cook noodles.
2. Ladle in fragrant broth and layer on bright toppings.

Sesame Chili Oil Ramen

Broth:

- 4 cups chicken or veggie broth
- 1 tbsp soy sauce
- 1 tsp sesame paste or tahini
- 1 tsp rice vinegar
- 1 tsp chili oil (or to taste)
- Optional: Sichuan peppercorn for numbing heat

Toppings:

- Ground pork or tofu (optional)
- Scallions
- Chili crisp
- Toasted sesame seeds
- Bok choy

Assembly:

1. Cook ramen noodles.
2. Pour spicy sesame broth, top with heat and crunch.

Soft Shell Crab Ramen

Broth:

- 4 cups seafood broth
- 1 tbsp soy sauce
- 1 tsp mirin
- Dash of yuzu or lime juice

Toppings:

- Tempura-fried soft shell crab
- Nori
- Pickled daikon
- Shiso leaf or scallions

Assembly:

1. Cook ramen noodles.
2. Place crispy crab on top just before serving for texture contrast.

Roasted Duck Miso Ramen

Broth:

- 4 cups duck or chicken stock
- 1 tbsp red miso
- 1 tsp hoisin sauce
- Garlic & ginger (sautéed)
- Whisk in miso at low heat

Toppings:

- Sliced roasted duck breast
- Bamboo shoots
- Soft-boiled egg
- Green onions
- Chili threads (optional)

Assembly:

1. Cook noodles.
2. Add savory miso broth, top with elegant roasted duck.

Bulgogi Beef Ramen

Broth:

- 4 cups beef broth
- 1 tbsp soy sauce
- 1 tsp sesame oil
- Garlic and ginger (optional)
- Simmer lightly

Bulgogi Beef:

- Marinate thin beef in soy, sugar, garlic, sesame oil
- Sear until caramelized

Toppings:

- Bulgogi beef
- Kimchi
- Green onions
- Soft-boiled egg
- Sesame seeds

Assembly:

1. Cook ramen noodles.
2. Ladle broth and add sweet-savory beef and bold toppings.

Charred Corn & Bacon Ramen

Broth:

- 4 cups chicken broth
- 1 tbsp soy sauce
- 1 tsp miso paste
- 1 tsp butter

Toppings:

- Charred corn (pan-roasted)
- Crisp bacon bits
- Soft-boiled egg
- Scallions
- Black pepper

Assembly:

1. Cook noodles.
2. Add buttery broth, top with smoky, sweet-salty toppings.

Ginger Scallion Ramen

Broth:

- 4 cups chicken or veggie broth
- 1-inch ginger (grated)
- 1 garlic clove
- 1 tbsp soy sauce
- Simmer and strain

Ginger Scallion Sauce:

- 2 scallions (minced)
- 1 tbsp ginger (minced)
- Salt
- Neutral oil (heated and poured over to sizzle)

Toppings:

- Sauce spooned on top
- Soft-boiled egg
- Baby bok choy
- Optional: crispy shallots or tofu

Assembly:

1. Cook noodles.

2. Add broth, spoon sauce generously over, and garnish.

Sake-Steamed Clam Ramen

Broth:

- 2 cups dashi
- 1 cup clam juice
- 1/2 cup sake
- 1 tbsp soy sauce
- 1 tsp mirin
- Simmer with clams until they open, then remove and strain.

Toppings:

- Sake-steamed clams
- Green onions
- Wakame seaweed
- Nori
- Lemon or yuzu zest

Assembly:

1. Cook ramen noodles.
2. Pour delicate ocean broth, top with juicy clams and aromatics.

Kimchi Cheese Ramen

Broth:

- 4 cups chicken or vegetable broth
- 1/2 cup chopped kimchi
- 1 tbsp gochujang
- 1 tsp soy sauce
- Simmer together

Toppings:

- Shredded mozzarella or cheddar
- More kimchi
- Soft-boiled egg
- Scallions
- Toasted sesame seeds

Assembly:

1. Cook noodles.
2. Pour spicy-tangy broth, top with a pile of melty cheese and kimchi.

Tempura Vegetable Ramen

Broth:

- 4 cups kombu or veggie broth
- 1 tbsp soy sauce
- 1 tsp mirin
- Light and clean base

Tempura:

- Slice vegetables (sweet potato, zucchini, eggplant)
- Dip in tempura batter, fry until crisp

Toppings:

- Tempura vegetables
- Grated daikon
- Green onions
- Nori strips

Assembly:

1. Cook ramen noodles.
2. Add broth, place tempura on top last to preserve crunch.

Oyster Cream Ramen

Broth:

- 2 cups light seafood broth
- 1/2 cup cream
- 1/4 cup sake
- 1 tbsp butter
- Gently blend in shucked oysters, simmer briefly

Toppings:

- Poached oysters
- Chives
- Microgreens
- Lemon zest
- Nori

Assembly:

1. Cook ramen noodles.
2. Pour in luxurious oyster cream, top with briny delicacies.

Roasted Tomato Basil Ramen

Broth:

- Roast: cherry tomatoes, garlic, onion, olive oil (400°F for 20 mins)
- Blend with 3 cups veggie broth
- Add 1 tbsp soy sauce, 1 tsp balsamic, and fresh basil

Toppings:

- More roasted tomatoes
- Fresh basil
- Parmesan or miso-parm crisp
- Olive oil drizzle
- Optional: mozzarella ball or burrata

Assembly:

1. Cook noodles.
2. Pour in savory-sweet roasted tomato broth and add fresh garden toppings.

Maple Miso Glazed Ramen

Broth:

- 4 cups chicken or vegetable broth
- 1 tbsp white miso
- 1 tsp soy sauce
- 1 tsp sesame oil
- Stir until smooth and heated through

Maple Glaze:

- 2 tbsp maple syrup
- 1 tbsp soy sauce
- 1/2 tsp garlic (minced)
- Simmer until slightly thickened

Toppings:

- Glazed roasted tofu or pork belly
- Roasted sweet potato cubes
- Green onions
- Toasted sesame seeds
- Soft-boiled egg

Assembly:

1. Cook ramen noodles.

2. Add miso broth, top with maple-glazed protein and cozy fall-inspired garnishes.

Chili Lime Chicken Ramen

Broth:

- 4 cups chicken broth
- 1 tbsp lime juice
- 1 tsp chili oil
- 1 garlic clove
- 1 tsp soy sauce

Chicken:

- Marinate chicken in chili powder, lime juice, garlic, salt
- Grill or pan-sear until juicy and charred

Toppings:

- Chili lime chicken slices
- Cilantro
- Lime wedge
- Corn kernels
- Pickled red onion

Assembly:

1. Cook ramen noodles.
2. Pour in zesty broth and add bold toppings for a bright, spicy bowl.

Garlic Butter Shrimp Ramen

Broth:

- 4 cups seafood or chicken broth
- 1 tbsp soy sauce
- 1/2 tbsp butter
- 1/2 tsp garlic powder
- Simmer gently

Shrimp:

- Sauté shrimp in butter and minced garlic until pink and fragrant

Toppings:

- Garlic butter shrimp
- Spinach or bok choy
- Scallions
- Lemon zest
- Chili flakes (optional)

Assembly:

1. Cook ramen noodles.
2. Add savory garlic butter broth, top with shrimp and greens.

Tofu & Avocado Ramen

Broth:

- 4 cups vegetable broth
- 1 tbsp white miso
- 1 tsp sesame oil
- 1/2 tsp rice vinegar
- Stir well, keep light and clean

Toppings:

- Cubed, pan-seared tofu
- Sliced ripe avocado
- Edamame
- Radish slices
- Microgreens
- Black sesame seeds

Assembly:

1. Cook ramen noodles.
2. Add mellow broth, arrange fresh toppings with a touch of creamy avocado.

Spicy Black Bean Ramen

Broth:

- 4 cups veggie broth
- 1/4 cup pureed black beans
- 1 tbsp soy sauce
- 1 tbsp chili garlic paste
- 1/2 tsp cumin
- Blend and simmer until smooth

Toppings:

- Crushed tortilla strips or fried shallots
- Sautéed black beans
- Scallions
- Corn
- Jalapeño slices
- Lime wedge

Assembly:

1. Cook ramen noodles.
2. Pour in bold black bean broth and garnish for a spicy, Latin-inspired ramen fusion.

www.ingramcontent.com/pod-product-compliance
Lightning Source LLC
LaVergne TN
LVHW081319060526
838201LV00055B/2375